The first Christmas

LITTLE – BIG BOOKS

by Gordon Stow

WORD BOOKS, PUBLISHER
WACO, TEXAS

FIRST PUBLISHED 1971

Scripture Union 5 Wigmore Street London W1H OAD

Many years ago
Mary and Joseph
went to Bethlehem.

They had to rest
in a stable,

And there,
Jesus, the Son of God,
was born.

Shepherds came
to worship Him,

And wise men
brought Him presents.

At Christmas we remember the birthday of Jesus.

You will find this story in Matthew chapters 1 and 2, and Luke chapters 1 and 2.